AFFILIATE MARKETING

Step by Step Guide to Learn All the Secrets About Affiliate Marketing

(How to Evaluate Whether You Should Pick a Product or Not)

Crystal Branch

Published by Oliver Leish

Crystal Branch

All Rights Reserved

Affiliate Marketing: Step by Step Guide to Learn All the Secrets About Affiliate Marketing (How to Evaluate Whether You Should Pick a Product or Not)

ISBN 978-1-77485-189-0

Legal & Disclaimer

The information contained in this book is not designed to replace or take the place of any form of medicine or professional medical advice. The information in this book has been provided for educational and entertainment purposes only.

The information contained in this book has been compiled from sources deemed reliable, and it is accurate to the best of the Author's knowledge; however, the Author cannot guarantee its accuracy and validity and cannot be held liable for any errors or omissions. Changes are periodically made to this book. You must consult your doctor or get professional medical advice before using any of the suggested remedies, techniques, or information in this book.

Upon using the information contained in this book, you agree to hold harmless the Author from and against any damages, costs, and expenses, including any legal fees potentially resulting from the application of any of the information provided by this guide. This disclaimer applies to any damages or injury caused by the use and application, whether directly or indirectly, of any advice or information presented, whether for breach of contract, tort, negligence, personal injury, criminal intent, or under any other cause of action.

You agree to accept all risks of using the information presented inside this book. You need to consult a professional medical practitioner in order to ensure you are both able and healthy enough to participate in this program.

Table of Contents

Introduction

You might be asking how is that possible. You might be asking. This is my life. This is a comprehensive guide to affiliate marketing.

Money might not be your main goal when you first begin to work with the idea of starting a blog. Take a look at how an average person gets up in the morning.

Each morning, I woke up at 6 AM to an annoying morning timer. Each morning, it was a struggle to get up.

To make sure that I didn't get stuck in traffic jams for an hour after I finally woke up, my morning routine had to be rushed.

At some point, I realized that I was working almost all my life to make another person wealthy.

The worst part was the encouragement from everyone that this was a normal way of life and that I should be thankful that I had a job I could rush to.

Did you ever feel there was more to life than just working and caring for tabs?

"9-5 is how you endure, and i ain't trying to endure

Jay - Z. I am trying to live it as much as possible and, more importantly, love it a lot.

Another option is available.

Imagine your body telling you to wake up naturally.

Your "drive" is a short walk or a change of clothes.

Sign in to a website and it shows that you have made hundreds of thousands of dollars overnight. Running over a decade now.

Continue reading and I will show you how.

It was in 2017.

It seems like everyone was making money from the internet.

YouTubers make 7-figures per year, you learn. Another multi-year-old geek makes a fortune from a startup.

After a few months, however the majority of people start to ask questions and wonder how they did it.

Affiliate marketing can help you to get the money you need for your passion and blog.

Some people make it big by blogging and selling affiliate marketing products.

Affiliate marketing can generate easy income, regardless of what many people say. However, this is not something that will make you wealthy sitting around doing nothing. You have to put in the work. This isn't a scam to make money; it's a great deal.

All the information available about SEO, blogging, email marketing and more can overwhelm you.

Affiliate marketing is an addition to the list. Yet, this book is written because of that. Its primary purpose is to dispel the myths surrounding affiliate marketing and monetizing blogs.

It's the guide that I wish I had when I started.

You have read this far and are now ready to learn more about affiliate marketing.

Let's get started!

Chapter 1: choosing a niche

If you are passionate about what you do, profiting online will seem easier than it is in real life. Many Internet marketers have learned that it is important to find a topic that interests you.

Imagine starting a dog grooming business even if you don't like dogs. A business will not reach its full potential if it lacks the love and energy that you put into it. You'll also become exhausted by it. You will find it more difficult to keep your business afloat if you are exhausted. Online businesses are no different.

Find a topic you are passionate about, or a theme you enjoy. There are many areas that you could focus on. You like pups? You might want to consider more specific breeds like the Chihuahua or pets. You can focus on one limb as well as dog health and care.

A mix of components will influence your decision about the business sector you choose.

Do you know the business well? You will reap a lot of energy, so choose a business that is exciting to you from the beginning.

What would you describe as your fascination with this business? Learning is an ongoing process. To stay current with industry trends and patterns, you must constantly upgrade your skills. To make your constant search for information more enjoyable and fulfilling, you should choose a market you are interested in.

What is your business's perspective? You wouldn't want to focus on a dying business sector where your products aren't being sold. A HUNGRY business is one that can support long-term benefits. We now get to the core of financial success...

What is the potential interest in this business sector? This is the first step to financial success, so it should be high.

How big is the opposition to the business? This is the second part of financial success: supply should be low.

Profitable market = Low supply and high demand

This is the ONLY FORMULA that you should remember when choosing a business. This is the foundation of financial success. It is the reason there are so many high-benefit organisations throughout history. High yielding ventures don't happen overnight.

These are the results of hard work and careful study. Everything starts with selecting the right isale sector for their ventures. You can focus on the variables using many online tools. Pick subjects that have high volumes of searches. My personal determinant is not less than 1,000,000 searches per month. This will ensure that I am not the only one who is truly interested in the subject. It is difficult to find a sub-theme that charges multiple ventures. Since you will be using the Internet, it is important to determine how many sites are involved.

You can search the sub-point on www.google.com. You can see the number of pages that appear in the top area of the results page. If the subject charges 1,000,000 searches per month and there are 2,000,000 sites supporting it, then the supply will exceed the interest and affiliate success in this field will be very slim. You can bet that if the subject charges 1,000,000 searches per month and there are only 2,000 sites supporting it, you will have a goldmine. This is how you find a large market on the World Wide Web.

Chapter 2: how to start affiliate marking thought a website?

Affiliate internet marketing doesn't require a website. Your site visitors will be directed directly to the product's gross sale web page.

This is not the best idea. You can earn much more income by directing potential customers to your order page with affiliate commissions.

Why is it so important for affiliate marketers to have a site?

This question can be answered legally by a few causes.

You can host your website and manage it yourself. You cannot shut it down or delete it at any time.

Many of their hard work has been lost without any reason. Your blog will likely be deleted without notice if you are spamming or using improper advertising techniques. You decide what you want to remove based on your specific area.

Pre-Sell to Your Customers

You should also pre-sell potential clients before you send them the link to the website where they can buy the affiliate products you sell. You can build a relationship by connecting with your readers. They will be more likely to purchase from you if they visit your site and find that they have experienced the same problem. It would be impossible to make this connection if you sent the email directly to the sales page.

Choose Your Best NICHE

Create your email list

You may be able to capture emails if you have a website that is related to the subject you are interested in.

This means that you can reach these people sooner or later to remind or provide them with complement merchandise that you could offer as an affiliate.

This will help you to promote the trusting relationship that you want to establish with your readers. Your entire process will be made easier by having an autoresponder connected to your opt-in form.

There are many reasons why a website is important if you're an associate marketer, as you can see.

If you decide to use a free blogging service, you are putting your online business at risk. They will immediately shut you down.

If you aren't connecting with site visitors or providing the correct resolution to their problems, cash may be left on the desk.

In return for their services or products being promoted, companies will happily pay you commissions.

If you choose the right area of interest and keep focused, you can make great earnings.

Three Highly Recommend Tools to Use When You Start A.. Marke ng?

Affiliate marketing is possible without any funding.

It may be easier to reduce your income and turn it into a full-blown paycheck if you spend many dollars for instruments that are extremely useful.

While they won't make you a better marketer, they can help increase traffic to your affiliate links and allow you to generate revenue almost immediately.

These are the three main tools that every affiliate marketer should have in their arsenal.

1. 1.

This is your website's address. You can have a great website or blog for free online. However, it is not common to find one that is beneficial.

You can't personalize your internet presence if you choose the accessible route. You can request that the firm offering the area be removed at any moment, with no reason.

It is vital that you have your own area title. You can purchase a website name that will help you get more site visitors through search engines if you have done your research correctly.

2. 2.

It is essential that your website joins website hosting in order to make it live alone. You can upload your website to an internet host and it will be visible around the globe. There are many internet hosting companies that offer so many options it can be confusing. It is a good idea to choose the right company to provide you with the plan that best suits your needs.

For a low monthly cost, Host Gator's Baby Plan is a great option for new and intermediate affiliate entrepreneurs. You can host unlimited domains in the same account, which has a one-month-to-month price.

SiteGround hosting has been a great choice for all my websites.

SiteGround is available for you to check out.

TRY HERE. (If you buy this product through my link, I may earn a commission at no additional cost to you.

3. Autoresponder

The majority of affiliate entrepreneurs are reluctant to invest in this instrument at the beginning. They regret it later, and wish they had listened to other entrepreneurs who suggested building an inventory.

Your personal email list will allow you to build a rapport with many people. To get them to believe you, you can offer them free content material. You can then advertise something they might find useful and you will reap the benefits. You can send emails to people who have signed up for the autoresponder and they will be added to your list.

To make your internet marketing more simple and straightforward, you should get a website, an internet hosting plan, as well as an autoresponder.

How To Choose A Pro table Niche For Af liate Marke ng?

It is important that you choose a segment that can earn you affiliate income. To make sure that they are important decisions, the niches you select must have many issues.

What Will Make Money?

It is best to only consider niches you are passionate about. Affiliate marketing online is not for everyone.

Web advertising is not the same as doing something you enjoy. It may be possible to make money in the subject area you choose, but it is not always easy.

It can seem overwhelming to think about all the affiliate products on the market.

What product type do you need to work with?

How to Choose the Best Product to Promote

Two fundamental options are available:

1. Digital and 2. Digital and 2.

Each type has its own pros and cons. It's worth taking the time to research all information before deciding which one you want to promote.

Digital Products

These include the repair and knowledge of any associated products that can be found online. These include eBooks, software programs and movies that clients have instant access to after they purchase. ClickBank and Warrior Plus are two of the most popular marketplaces to promote these products.

Sign up to ClickBank

Pros and Cons of Digital Products

It is easy to set up accounts and start selling. There is no need for the client or the client to be present on the product being shipped.

Cons of Digital Products

Owners of product houses might lose their website or go offline at any moment. Refunds can sometimes be more generous for digital products. Those with electronic mailing lists are more likely to be successful than competitors. It may be harder to convert browsers into customers. Can be paid weekly, bi-weekly.

Physical Products

These are the items you can purchase at Walmart or another retailer. You can sell many options in the identical area of interest if you have bodily merchandise. Many of your readers will be looking for reviews on this product so that they can make an informed purchase.

Many people choose the Amazon Affiliate Program for online bodily products.

Pros of Physical Products

There are many niches and options to choose from. It might be more reliable to work with large corporations than digital product house owners.

Cons of Physical Products

These merchandise are more difficult to market without a website. It is also less expensive (often 5%-10%).

Chapter 3: select the right affiliate networks

We promoted an offer in the wealth niche under the topic "Proven methods to make money online" in our previous example.

There are many affiliate networks you can choose to join. These are the ones I recommend. These are all fantastic networks, and I have tried them all. They all have user-friendly features and great support staff.

My favourite networks are Amazon, Warriorplus and Warriorplus because I have earned excellent affiliate commissions from them.

* Amazon Associates

* Warriorplus

* JVZoo

* Clickbank

Register to join an affiliate network

My goal is to promote make money online in the wealth niche. The best networks for this are Warriorplus and JVZoo.

Amazon Associates is a great way to promote physical products.

You will learn how to get links from Clickbank and Warriorplus. Clickbank is the easiest because you don't need to be approved by the vendor to promote their products. Once you feel comfortable with the process, you can experiment with other networks.

Once you have mastered the system, you are able to apply it to any network or affiliate offer you choose.

Go to warriorplus.com now and create an account, if you don't already have one. Signing up is easy. I already have an account so I won't create another. Follow the steps below to get started.

Fill in the details and click "Free Signup".

For payment details, I recommend that you open a Paypal account. They will deposit your affiliate commissions and refunds from this account. Signing up for Paypal is easy. To create an account, go to paypal.com

To make it easier to promote affiliate offers, I recommend you sign up for all of the networks I have previously listed. You can create an account for free.

Select the Right Offer to Promote

You can start promoting once you have an account at Warriorplus!

Once you log in to your dashboard, you'll see the top 10 daily offers.

Because these top 10 offers are brand new, you may choose to promote them. You must be prepared to compete with other affiliates, as they may also be promoting the same offer.

If you don't want to miss out, visit the offers section to see other evergreen offers. "Evergreen" refers to offers that are always in high demand and can be used.

Click "affiliate" and then "offers".

You can view all of the current offers, from old to new. You would naturally want to promote only evergreen and fresh products.

The rule of thumb

Always consider the following criteria when choosing an offer. This will allow you to pick the most profitable offer right away!

* Launch Date - It should not exceed 3 months from the date of launch, unless it's an evergreen product.

* Sales should not be less than 1000

* Conversion rate - Must be at least 10%

* Visitor Value should not be less than $5

* Average Sales - Not that Important

* The refund rate must not exceed 5%

* Pulse is not so important

Send us your request for an affiliate link

In this instance, I will be promoting "5iphon Reloaded Pro".

Click on the "Request" tab in the upper right corner of the screen to get your unique affiliate link. Next, click "Request Approval".

Before we move on, please click "View Sales Page" to view the details of the product.

This is where you will find the benefits and features of the offer. We are going to use this to create the description for our YouTube video.

Here's the sales page for the product:

When you click the "Request approval", you will need to choose your Paypal account. Next, send a message to the vendor describing how you plan to promote their product.

Do not make outrageous claims. Be real and honest.

It will be difficult for a newbie to be approved by most vendors. However, most vendors will approve you if they feel you are genuine and honest.

Copy and paste the following message to make your case more convincing and ensure approval.

"I am a customer _____ (any product that you have purchased before). I will promote your offer on my Youtube channel _____. I will only send quality leads and not spam. I am willing to accept delayed commissions.

Copy the following into the "Request Notes" field.

As shown above, click the blue "Request an Offer" button.

The next step is to wait for them to approve your request. After you have been approved, you will receive your unique link. Then you can promote and earn money! You can also find more information here:

Approval can take anywhere from 1-3 days. Be patient.

Clickbank.com is the other network I'll show you. Go to this website and create an account. It is easy to sign up, just like Warriorplus.

Click "Create an Account".

Please fill out the form below. Please fill out the form correctly, including banking information.

Once you have created an account, go to clickbank.com's homepage and log in.

Log in with the username and password that you have created during sign-up.

You will see your dashboard, which shows you all of your weekly and daily sales snapshots.

For obvious reasons, I kept my username and profits secret.

Click on "Marketplace", as seen above.

The next screen will show all categories in the left-hand menu.

Start taking your time to get familiar with the platform. It's very easy to use and navigate.

You can choose to enter any offer that you wish to promote in the "Find Products" field.

Instead of typing it, I recommend you just leave it blank and then click the search button.

It will display all top-selling Clickbank offers in an order.

Always consider the "Gravity" of any offer when choosing an offer. This will show you how many affiliates have promoted and made money from the offer. Don't be afraid to compete. This is a sign that the offer is highly converting. Once you get started promoting it, you will be able to have a share of the large pie.

The "Flat Belly Fix", offer, shows an extremely high gravity of 198.53.

This simply means that the product is highly converting and tons of affiliates make money by promoting it.

Our example will use keywords that are about making money online. Let's look for offers that match this theme.

Continue to page 2, and so on, until you find what you are looking for.

After searching, I came across "Super Affiliate System", which offered $499.64 per sale. It is related to the keywords "make money online through affiliate marketing". This is a great deal that could make you a lot of cash with just a few sales.

It has a gravity value of 62.68, and it also offers a recurring income. It is a good rule of thumb to always promote offers that offer recurring income. This will help you to build a passive income for many years.

Anything above 50 is a good gravity level to promote. The greater the gravity, the better.

Click "promote" and enter your username and password.

Although you can choose from any of these landing pages, in this instance we will stick with the default.

Click "Generate Hoplinks".

This is

Now, create your unique affiliate link to promote the offer. It can be saved on a notepad.

If you notice, your affiliate link is quite long. Site bitly.com can help you make your affiliate link shorter. This site will reduce the length of your links and hide your affiliate link. This is a free service that you don't have to pay for. You can find it here:

Copy and paste the link, then click "Shorten".

This will provide you with the shorter link. It's shorter and more attractive.

It can be saved somewhere. This is what you'll use to promote your products.

We have now chosen the offer we wish to promote, and obtained our affiliate link. The fun part is now - making money with the promotions!

You don't have to film your videos or put your face in front of the camera. There's a shortcut. It is easy to do.

Chapter 4: what is affiliate marketing?

Affiliate marketing is when a company promotes its product/service with the assistance of another party. A commission is paid to another company for promoting products and/or services and securing sales for the original company. The affiliate marketing process involves three parties.

The Advertiser (or Merchant). This person is responsible for selling the product/service. The other party must agree to promote and sell the product or service.

The Marketer (or Marketer). The Publisher or Marketer is the party who promotes the Advertiser's product/service. The Advertiser will provide text ads, banners, links or any other assistance needed to link a consumer to the Advertiser's transaction web page. This is not a free service. As compensation for services, the Marketer can expect a commission. This could be a percentage or a dollar amount. An ID will be issued by the Advertiser to an affiliate for the purpose recording and tracking any owed commissions.

The Consumer. Responding to the Call to Action on the Marketer's website. The individual who completes a conversion to buy the Advertiser's product/service.

Internet technology is the heart of the relationship between the Advertiser and Marketer. It is important to keep track of how many Consumers have contacted the Advertiser through the Marketer. Cookies are used to do this. The cookie stores information. The cookie embedded in the banner advertisement or text link on the Marketer's website will track when the consumer clicked on the promotional information. Affiliate marketing uses a first-party cookie. This cookie will identify the Marketer and the Advertiser and, most importantly, the Marketer's commission.

A. A.

The cyber economy has enabled the creation of new commercial entities that were not possible just a few years ago. Affiliate marketing is not possible with every one. However, there are many that can be used to help affiliate marketers succeed.

1. Social networks. Social media can make shopping easy. Good networks will have retail links that improve the user experience and also generate money. It is wise to inform those who use the network about affiliate marketing.

2. Coupon sites and sales. They can be paid a commission for every purchase made through promotions. A sales and coupon website must adhere to any IAB guidelines. These sites can generate a lot of traffic, which is why merchants will want to work with them.

3. Forums. These forums are not just for political debate. These forums include

peer reviews that can influence purchases. The community's opinions can help you make more money with affiliate marketing.

4. Blogs. Bloggers value content. Many commercial blogs will post reviews and promote products. Bloggers may adapt their content to promote a particular advertiser. There is very little chance that an advertiser will have a dominant role in editing content. Consumers looking to purchase can find help from bloggers. In many ways, affiliate marketing was created for bloggers.

B. B.

Anyone who is considering affiliate marketing should have a clear idea of the income stream. Although this can be a great way to make a lot of money, you need to be realistic and cautious. This is not El Dorado, or the Lost Dutchman's Mine. It is possible to lose some money in the beginning. STM Forum did a survey of its members a few years back to see how financially they were doing with affiliate marketing. The survey revealed that 19% of respondents were earning $20,000 or less. Affiliate marketing is a lucrative way to make $200,000 per year, according to just over half the respondents. About 17% of respondents said that they were major players who made $1 million or more. The median income is between $81,000 and $220,000 annually.

Affiliate marketing isn't a conservative model of economic growth. It can be volatile and you could make nothing one day but earn a few hundred dollars the next. According to the STM Forum survey, the median figure was $221 to $328 per day. Good news is that affiliate marketing isn't a week-end but a year. You can make money every single day with your program. How you manage activity will determine how much.

It is important to be realistic in your expectations. It is not realistic to expect that you will consistently make $1,000 per day. Profit generation is dependent on traffic. While a person at the lowest level of affiliate marketing will not generate large amounts of money, they are not likely to take on significant risk. Another thing to keep in mind is that the greater your risk, the more profit you will make if you actually generate cash.

An entrepreneur who is smart will adopt the mindset of a long-distance runner. It will take time and perseverance. The idea of a quick scheme to make money is not something you should be doing. To make affiliate marketing profitable, you will need to have some strategy sessions. It is important to know the best niche to work in and how to draw people to your site. It is also important to have an idea of the income you can expect to earn over a certain period. As you create long-term revenue streams, it is important to be realistic. While we'll be covering all of these, it was important to know upfront how much money you were looking at when you use affiliate marketing.

Consider the above figures. For promoting someone else's products or services, even $100 or $200 per day can be a good amount of revenue. It is not possible to guarantee that affiliate marketing will allow you to quit your job. It is clear that affiliate marketing can bring in a significant income if it is done correctly. You may be able to make a good income as an affiliate marketer if you work at.

Although the possibilities are endless, affiliate marketing isn't magic. Without the right affiliates, income will not be generated. It is also important to make some decisions about how the website will be promoted by affiliates. Some people are more inclined to do the entire work. This is fine, but may be inefficient. Writing content is a skill that many people have and should be able to focus on it. These marketers will hire a third party to help with the setup of an affiliate marketing program. This is a good thing. It is better to outsource the things you don't know and focus more on what you do. It can improve quality, which in turn will lead to the desired levels of commission.

C. Various Strategies

You can't just wait for traffic to become an affiliate marketer if you want to make it big. While you may attract a few people who are interested, you need to be able drive the numbers that will lead to the commissions you desire. Concentrate on the ideas that will attract interested consumers.

Review Products. Review Products. People are always interested in consumer opinions. This is where your writing skills can be put to use. Marketers are in high demand from affiliate marketers. You would decide what niche you will focus on and then start writing reviews about products. Because the Internet marketplace is becoming more sophisticated, you must be as trustworthy as possible when writing reviews. Poor reviews can be easily detected by people. If you have a bad reputation for writing useless reviews, you will not get the traffic that you want. An honest review will convince people to go to the transaction page on your advertiser's site.

Make an email list. An email list is the best way to encourage visitors to return to your site. You are basically asking visitors if they would like to receive updates on product reviews and other information from your website. An e-book is a great way to get an email address. They don't have to be as large as a college textbook. Most e-books contain between 7000 to 15,000 words. The e-book can be offered for free on your website. All the interested parties need to do is enter their email address to get the document. This will give you an email address that you can use to notify people about new products and new content on the website. It is a good idea to ask the person if they are okay with reminding people. This is polite and you will know that the person has more interest than a passing one in your work.

What about a Webinar? We have to admit that this is quite ambitious but it's the logic. You may have seen different products promoted at a county or state fair. This can be quite entertaining, but it also allows salespeople to reach a lot of potential customers. They find it far more rewarding than cold calling. They use the opportunity to showcase all the great qualities of a product. The same can be done for you. A webinar can be promoted on social media and streamed live via Google Hang Out. This will allow you to promote the product to a large audience. Webinars allow you to introduce yourself to your audience. You become more than a name on a website. This is the type of contact that can help you build a relationship and collect commissions.

PPC advertising (also known as pay-per-click advertising) is a way to reach people. However, this requires that you are able to pay for the advertisement. We recommend that you do not get too complicated until the revenue starts coming in. You can save the money for later use as we mentioned. In a matter of months, you may find yourself using PPC advertising.

D. Avoid Making Mistakes

Affiliate marketing is a new field and beginners will make mistakes. They won't ruin you, but they could limit your profitability and make it harder for you to get the income you desire. These are the most common mistakes that you should avoid.

Don't be a high-pressure salesperson. It is not your goal to sell the product, but to guide people to further information about it. You can use a calmer call to action. Your chances of an Internet consumer clicking through to your advertiser are higher if you present yourself as an impartial third party.

Do Not Overdo It. You may not need every affiliate program. You can make your website look horrible with many affiliate programs. While you are trying to make some money, you will find that many of these affiliates only pay small commissions. Other affiliates, however, may have higher commission rates and be in the same niche as you. These are the best.

Make sure to do some testing. This means that you should put yourself in the shoes of a customer responding to an affiliate ad on your website. How is the vendor responding? You can see how someone else feels if they receive too many emails from this vendor and why they might not trust your website.

Tracking is important. Tracking affiliate links are important for your website. This allows you to track the source of the sale. This will allow you to determine which pages of your website are converting the most.

It is important to stay focused. Don't be distracted by all the shiny and bright affiliate programs. Focus on a handful of them and learn from your mistakes. Again, novices try to diversify their options by trying many different ideas. It's better to focus on just a few campaigns rather than trying to do everything.

Google is your best friend. Google does not want honest businesses to be hampered by tricks and games. Google offers guidance that every affiliate marketer should follow. Google recommends that you exercise caution when looking at the various affiliate programs. While not all affiliate programs are scammy, many offer great business opportunities. You'd be smart to review Google's guidelines when you want to check out what's being offered online.

Chapter 5: how to start an online business today

It is nearly impossible to live a meaningful and fulfilling life without making money, regardless of whether you are earning money from a business or a job.

Most students realize that they need to specialize in a subject that prepares them for the job market as soon as they enter High School. Students must plan how they will continue making money after they leave college. Making money is essential for survival and independence. People must be creative in this regard.

Online is arguably the fastest and easiest way to make money. In recent years, many people have created very successful online businesses that have staff members and clients all around the globe. Online businesses are very accessible to anyone who has access to the internet.

Like any other business field, online businesses offer the possibility of a wide range of options. While some may be more lucrative than others, there are still many that are viable. Below is a list of some of the most lucrative online businesses, as well as those you can start right away.

How do you make money online in a month?

It is supposed to be amazing to make money online. It can, and it is possible. There are however some truths that everyone should be aware of. People can make money online by:

Earn a decent income

Start without much capital

You can take control of their lives, and their time.

They can wear whatever they like

They can work whenever they like, even in their pajamas

You can work from your home

Help many people

It can be very entertaining

Travel with your employees and work while you travel

Many people believe that online work means they can own their business, make lots of money, travel first-class, take expensive holidays and drive expensive cars. They expect to make quick money online. Most people give up on their dreams after only a few weeks.

As with any business, it is difficult to run an online business. While there are many people making a lot of money online, they often put in a lot more effort, patience, time, and effort to succeed. This should not discourage or scare anyone. Instead, this should encourage people to believe in their abilities and to work harder to achieve their dreams. There are few things more satisfying than earning a living from your home or while traveling.

You can easily search online for online businesses to find many sites. Most of these are quick ways to make money. Most of these schemes don't work. It is impossible to make a living online without hard work and a few nights of sleepless nights. Online businesses like affiliate marketing are great because they can be operated 24/7. One can still make some hard cash even if one is asleep.

One of the best things about online money making is the possibility to fall in love with it. It can also be very addictive. It can be difficult to take a break, which is a problem. It is easy to become overwhelmed by all the online information. This is unhealthy. They don't get enough sleep, eat well, or spend time with friends and family.

This is a rare exception. Online earning money is possible. It is possible for anyone to make their dream come true, even if it takes a month. There are many ways to make money online in a matter of a month:

Affiliate Marketing

This method is proven and tested to make money online. Many people make money online within days of their first start. Affiliate marketers work with brands and businesses within their niche blogs or websites. They link to a product or service they have searched for using an affiliate code that they received when they joined the program. They then earn money every time someone purchases a program or service through their link.

To make more money, you should join affiliates related to your website. For example, people with financial knowledge should concentrate their affiliate marketing efforts on products and services like savings accounts, credit cards, investment accounts, and credit cards. To get a better understanding of the best affiliate marketing strategies, it is a good idea to join multiple affiliate networks. There are many reputable affiliate networks out there that connect affiliate marketers with companies looking to sell their products or services.

Google AdSense

It is hard to miss Google ads when browsing the Internet. Because they are so easy to set up, they are all over the Internet. They can still be very profitable once a website or blog has a lot of traffic. Google AdSense is available to anyone who has a blog or website. Google AdSense is easy to use. All you have to do is paste the code provided by Google onto your website or blog.

Consulting

Experts in any field can make money online by doing this. Businesses and individuals are willing to pay experts to help them with certain tasks. These experts can be paid by large companies, sometimes at a staggering rate.

Find freelance clients and sell services

Freelancing is a way for people with marketable skills such as web design, writing, marketing and designing to make money in a matter of days. Although it may not be as scalable as other online income streams, it can still provide an opportunity to make extra money. Millions of people today are choosing to work for freelancing businesses over traditional jobs.

Start a YouTube Channel

YouTube is the most popular search engine in the world and anyone who can reach the minimum of 4,000 hours view time and 1000 subscribers within the last year can make money with it. The bottom line is that YouTube makes more money the more you view it. One can earn between $2 and $4 for every 1,000 views on YouTube. People who have videos that reach millions of views often laugh at the idea. After being approved by the site's partner programme, users can add ads to their videos.

You can also make money online in a matter of a month by doing these:

Part-time work for remote companies

Podcasts are a way to share inspiring content

Narrating audiobooks

Test websites

Micro-jobs

Influencers on Instagram

Facebook ads

Dropshipping

Online car rental

Online Forex trading

There are many opportunities today to make money online. You can't just leave your computer at home and expect to make a lot of money. You must put in the effort to learn and experiment in order to succeed with an online business.

The Most Successful Online Businesses

Online businesses are growing rapidly. While some people are doing exceptionally well, others struggle to survive. The online market for business is changing rapidly due to increasing consumer awareness and rapid technological advancements. Traditional businesses are now looking to expand their reach into the online marketplace, as it offers greater convenience and better reach.

It isn't as simple as people think to understand the online market. Affiliate marketers and online entrepreneurs need to possess certain traits in order to reap the rewards of the internet market. A positive reputation is key to any online business' success. It takes more than selling a product to become a successful affiliate marketer. Because most people have greater control today, it is important to make sure that everyone knows you are an authority in your niche.

Many people don't like their jobs. The internet is a great way to make money. Online businesses offer many personal and professional benefits. It can even be very exciting to achieve something new. More people are now doing business online in the digital age. Online businesses make a lot of money. They don't have to worry about being stuck in traffic on their way to work, renting or buying premises, or worrying about other things.

The Key Features of Online Businesses

A few things should be considered by anyone who is considering starting an online company. Online business is a smart choice due to the many benefits it offers. Online business isn't just for Amazon and eBay. Smaller businesses can also make great profits online. These businesses have some key characteristics:

Money Savings

This is one advantage to running an online business. Individuals can save on expenses like rent or purchase of a base for operation and travel costs. An online business can be a great option for those with limited funds.

Convenient, easy and simple

It can be difficult to start and run a business. However, an online business can be a great way to save yourself the stress and hassle of running a business. Many startups have chosen to go online as their sole source of income.

Perfect for niche products or services

For niche services or products, it is easy to do business online. Access to niche products and services is easier through the internet, which allows business owners to reach more customers. Affiliate marketers can help companies that sell specialty products and services reach a wider audience and increase their sales.

Popularity

People want to shop online 24/7, and this convenience is more important than ever. Online businesses can therefore cater to this increasing consumer demand.

Global Reach

Online businesses can reach a worldwide audience by operating online. However, traditional brick-and-mortar businesses have a limited audience. Online expansion can make a business more global.

Capability to measure and track

Online businesses have the advantage of being able to quickly track and measure their results, something that is not possible with traditional businesses. Online marketing allows businesses to use different tools to track their results, giving them insight into what is working and what isn't.

Multitasking ability

Online business offers many benefits, including the ability to manage multiple customers simultaneously through one website. A business website designed well can facilitate multiple transactions simultaneously and seamlessly. These types of businesses are able to adapt quickly and be successful.

Round-the-Clock Business

Online businesses can be run around the clock and are much cheaper to operate. Online businesses are more flexible than traditional brick-and-mortar businesses in terms of hours of operation. The issue of overtime pay is not an issue for employees. Online businesses do not require that you adapt to local or international time differences.

Instant Service

Online transactions are easy and quick. It is possible to use a digital payment service such as PayPal, which acts as a third-party and facilitates transactions between the buyer and seller.

Time-Effective

Online businesses are much easier to set up than traditional businesses. Online businesses are easy to set up and can be operated at their convenience. Depending on what type of job they choose, you can work online in a matter of hours. Anyone can sign up for an affiliate program with just minutes if they have a blog or website.

There are many reasons why running an online business has proven to be more profitable than ever before. The main reason is the increased demand for online services and products. Modern technology has made online transactions more efficient, simpler, and faster.

How to get started in affiliate marketing

Many people dream of starting an online business, or making extra income with an online side-hustle. Affiliate marketing is one of the fastest and easiest ways to make money online. Affiliate marketing can be used to increase income for existing businesses. Affiliate marketing, as the name suggests, is a marketing strategy in which brands or companies pay a commission for traffic or sales generated by their referrals.

It is possible to make it work with several strategies. For example, a blogger can become an affiliate marketer through an eCommerce company or an affiliate network. This will allow them to make an income by placing a banner or button within their blog posts that will direct readers to the company's products or services. Smart bloggers will also use multiple marketing strategies to promote their content.

Many affiliate marketers are successful. Unfortunately, many affiliate websites are not as successful due to too many ads and poor content. Affiliate marketers must be:

Organised

Sociable

Consistent

Official

Patient

Are you interested?

Things to Avoid

Content creation should be approached by affiliate marketers as if it were explaining something to a close friend. Writers shouldn't be portrayed as salespeople or change their tone. They should not make their blog look like a commercial, even though they are trying to sell something. It is best to discuss how the product or service helped them in relation to the topic of the blog post.

They should also avoid placing the banner, button or link in the blog in a way they don't understand. Instead, they should provide some kind of introduction or other information about the link before it is displayed so that it flows seamlessly and makes sense. A Federal Trade Agreement requires affiliate marketers to disclose their affiliations on all pages that have affiliate links.

How affiliate marketers make money

Affiliate marketing is one the most lucrative online businesses. This is something that many people don't know. It can be very lucrative if it is set up correctly. Affiliate marketers make money by receiving commissions from the brands they represent. Affiliate marketers can also make money through an affiliate-marketing program. Their user identification is included on the product or services banners, links or buttons that are placed on their websites. When users click on them, they will be able to choose to buy the product or service. The company will also know the identity and name of the affiliate who referred the customers. The affiliate will receive a commission.

How do I get started?

Choose a niche

To get started, you need to find a niche that is both broad and narrow. For example, golf. The market for male golfers between 20 and 25 years old is too small, while the market for "sports" is too big. It is important to choose a niche that is narrow enough to reach one's target audience, but broad enough to make money. It is also important to have the right knowledge, passion, and expertise in your niche. This passion will be a lifesaver during good and bad times. You must:

Analyze trends related to your niche

To get a better idea of what people are searching for online, conduct keyword research

Learn about the products and services that are available

Learn from the top brand influencers

Join affiliate networks and programs

67

Once you have chosen the niche that interests you, it is time to search for affiliate opportunities in that niche. There are many options. There are many affiliate programs that you can join, and they come in all shapes and sizes. Walmart, Target and Amazon are just a few of the large companies that offer affiliate programs. You need to market to a specific niche. However, it is important to find the right programs for you.

On the other hand, affiliate networks offer marketers access to many brands and companies that offer programs. These networks manage individual brand terms and conditions, so marketers don't have to deal directly with multiple programs.

It is crucial to know:

How to make money

Find the most profitable niche product or service to be an affiliate.

Create the affiliate-marketing platform

This is where affiliate links will be placed for products and services that you are marketing. It is easiest to do this through a blog or website. However, you can also promote your links via social media.

Make content

Now it's time to start creating great content to add weight to your niche. You can embed affiliate links in the content. There are many types of content you can use to promote affiliate products and services.

Review of product

Banner ads and sidebar

Get Discounts and Giveaways

Recipes

Fashion posts and style

DIY guides

Virtual store pages

Marketing Affiliate Offers

To market their affiliate products, affiliate marketers can use many different methods. These include email marketing, podcasting, video marketing and mobile apps.

Reselling vs Affiliates

Affiliates   Selling

You cannot market products or services under your own brand.   Sell products and services under your own brand

Get started for free   Start-up costs are low

Low level of service and responsibility   Service with high quality and less work

Total control of one's own business   Man cannot have complete control of one's business

Only commission sales   Price cannot be matched

Online business is extremely competitive. Nothing is easy. Affiliate marketing is no different. The benefits of this business line outweigh any negatives. To succeed, you must put in effort and take the time to learn.

Why Affiliate Marketing is the best online business to start

Internet has made a huge impact on the business world. Millions of people around the globe are now able to work from their homes, with the convenience and freedom that comes with it. Individuals and businesses can market their products and services worldwide without having to invest in additional staff or offices. Anyone with a flair for entrepreneurship can set up an online business and make a decent living.

Affiliate marketing is an excellent online business for making money. This business is highly attractive due to its unique benefits. Affiliate marketing allows anyone to start small and build an empire. Although it is a great way to make a few extra dollars, many people soon realize that affiliate marketing can be a lucrative business. This can be a great way to make money for ambitious people, stay-at-home parents, and anyone looking to make a lot of money each month.

You can start a blog to sell products and services online. While many affiliate marketers have been successful, they began by doing all the work themselves. However, once they had a large enough business, they started outsourcing a lot of the work. They put in a lot time, passion and effort to be successful.

It is the best online business because of these reasons

It's cheap

Affiliate marketing does not require a large budget. Many affiliate programs are free. Therefore, marketing and/or referrals of products or services will account for the majority of your operational costs. Even those costs can be reduced if you do your marketing properly.

It's easy to get started

Anyone can find the best affiliate networks, create a website or blog, learn how traffic is attracted, market their product or service and then wait for the money. Affiliate marketing is simpler than many people believe. You only need patience, passion, some time, and effort.

Workers can work anywhere

Affiliate marketers can work anywhere in the world. They can work as hard or as little as they like, at any hour of the day. It is a great alternative to the 9am-5pm workdays, irritating traffic, formal attire, and difficult to please bosses. You can work from your home, on a bench at the park, on the beach or in comfort. Internet access is all that's required.

It is not necessary to create a product or service.

Affiliate marketing doesn't require you to produce a product or provide support. Affiliate programs are offered by brands and businesses. Instead of worrying about the logistics and responsibilities involved in creating a product or service, one can simply focus on marketing one's site. You don't even need to ship products.

This is a great way to quickly make money.

Affiliate marketing is one way to make quick money online. Many people make money in a matter of months. It will make money if you are persistent enough to keep it working for you. It can make money all day.

Affiliate marketing is flexible

This type of business creates a workspace wherever you are and whenever you want. It allows people to build their own empires however they like. For example, if an emergency arises, one doesn't need to ask permission or explain to his boss the next day. Instead, one can just continue where one left off.

You don't need formal education.

A college degree is not required to become an affiliate marketer. It is easy to set up and run this type of business. Anyone can start an affiliate marketing business.

There is no limit to the potential for growth

It doesn't matter if you want to make passive income, or build a business with great websites. The possibilities for growth are endless and so is the potential to make a lot of money. The sky is the limit when it comes to income.

Affiliate marketing is a way for anyone to make money. Like any income-generating venture that generates income, success is dependent on how consistent and correct one acts. Affiliate marketing offers many advantages as a startup business venture.

Chapter 6: how to create the right website type to drive traffic

When they start their affiliate marketing website, not everyone is familiar with the process. A large portion of your time as an affiliate marketer will be spent creating promotional content, long-term relationships and pushing yourself to go the extra mile to make your content stand apart from other content. It's not just about SEO to create a website that drives profitable sales. There are many factors to consider.

To be a successful affiliate marketer, you must know how to effectively market yourself. You will need to attract thousands of people to your website if you are to become a full-time marketing professional. To do this, you must be well versed in the best ways to promote yourself to the world. It takes time and dedication to achieve this goal.

WordPress is a great platform to start a website. It's easy to use and affordable. This guide will help you understand WordPress and how it works. WordPress services are free, but you will need to pay for web hosting and domain name.

Domain Name - This is the URL that people use to reach your website. A domain registrar will be required to register your unique domain name. Although the terms may seem daunting, the process is easy.

Web Hosting - A web hosting service allows you to make your website available to the rest world. You are basically renting a web server.

These are two of the most important aspects to consider when building an affiliate marketing website. There are many places that offer these services at no cost, but it is best to avoid those services if you're serious about affiliate marketing. You might find that the site you approach for these services may even have a portion of your content. This doesn't sound very appealing, does it? To put it another way, your business, which you have spent so much time building, might not be entirely yours. You will also have complete control of everything when you own your website.

If you don't know where to begin, this step-by-step guide will help.

Step 1: Choose a good domain name

It is important to take time when choosing your domain name. If your domain name is not chosen well, it can limit the potential of your website in the future. If you choose topaudiogadgets.com, your niche will automatically be restricted to audio gadgets. You wouldn't want this for your website. Your website name might not allow you to review an air conditioner if you decide to revisit it in a few months. Thetechadvisor.com is a great resource because you can review any product related to tech. If you want your business to succeed in the future, your top priority should be long-term planning.

These are some things to remember when choosing a domain name for your site.

It should be simple to type. The longer the domain is, the more difficult it is for your audience's to remember. It should be short, simple, and easy to remember. Multiple spellings can also cause confusion in the minds of your audience. Some people might write 'express' in their domain names as 'xpress. This may sound cool at first, but your audience will not be able to spell it correctly and end up landing on a different website.

Names should contain appropriate keywords. There are many ways to come up with names that fit your website. You can start by choosing something that is related to your business, or the product category you are writing about. You can also base your website on the name of your business. However, strong keywords would play an important role. It is smart to use keywords in domain names. It has many SEO benefits. It is possible to rank your website higher in search engine results. Including keywords in the domain name can help you achieve that goal faster. Using the keywords potential in your domain name will allow any visitor to your website to instantly find out what your niche is.

A domain generator is available - If you run out of ideas, you can leave the task to brainstorming to a generator. You can only take names that haven't been taken before. You cannot, for example, name your blog thewirecutter.com if the name is already taken.

Avoid using numbers and hyphens - When you're brainstorming ideas, hyphens can cause confusions. If you say that your website's name is top10products.com then someone listening might mistakenly think it is toptenproducts.com. They would then not be able find your website.

It is important to choose the right domain name extension. The extensions at your domain name's end also play a part (.com,.net, etc.). Although the most common extension is.com, it can be difficult to find a catchy and short name for a.com extension. These are just a few of the extensions that are used most often, but they also have their own meanings:.me (for personal websites and blogs), www.non-commercial organizations,.org (for non-profits and other organizations that are not commercial in nature),.net (for websites related to technology-based subjects), and.info (for websites that are primarily informational)..co is used for abbreviations of words such as community, commerce, and more commonly, company.

Step 2 - Purchase Your Domain Name

After you have chosen the domain name and verified that it is available for purchase, you can move on to the next step. You have many options when it comes to the companies that you can purchase your domain from. HostGator is one of the most reputable domain registrars. A2 Hosting, Bluehost and Pantheon are also major registrars.

Select any website that interests you and then type the domain name into their search panel. It will immediately tell you if the name is available. If the name is available, you will need to proceed and pay the required fees. The domain will then be yours. You will need to provide some information to register the domain to your name. The next step after you have purchased the domain is to obtain web hosting.

Step 3 - Select a good web hosting company

If your web hosting isn't right, quality content won't be created. Your website's responsiveness will depend on how well your web hosting works. Forbes contributor James Lyne stated that over 30,000 websites are being hacked every day. Do you know why? All of them made bad choices regarding web hosting. There is no solution, but it is possible to be more cautious to avoid such problems. You can be sure that your web hosting company will keep their database up-to-date so they are prepared for any possible threats.

Here are some tips to help you make an informed decision when choosing a web hosting company.

You can narrow down your web hosting options by analyzing your specific business needs. If you plan to launch a review site with affiliate links and high-quality videos, your web hosting provider will need to be responsive. A shared server is not suitable for websites that are likely to get a lot of traffic. Only websites with a set list of requirements are compatible with shared servers.

It is crucial to choose the right hosting package. Many people start with shared hosting plans because they are cheaper and more affordable than those who don't want or need to invest a lot. However, they come with greater risks. These shared hosting plans have the biggest disadvantage of slow website response times. This could cause your visitors to lose patience and not be able to wait for your website to load. VPS, or Virtual Private Servers, can offer much better performance.

Before you settle for a company, read the reviews. Just like with any product, it would be a mistake to make a decision without reading the reviews. These reviews indicate how reliable the websites are. You can read reviews and see if there are any complaints or suggestions from users.

You need to choose the right bandwidth. You should always choose a bandwidth limit that allows for future growth. You should also verify that the web hosting company offers flexible options for upgrading your hosting plan in the future. You can always move up if your business requires it.

Do not fall for a lower price. It is easy to be tempted by hosting companies that offer cheaper rates when you're just starting out. You should avoid falling for this trap. Do not get caught up in the price. These companies don't do anything for free. These companies will charge less, so they will provide poorer service. This could be anything from a slower server to unresponsive customer service, or constant downtime.

Do not skim the Terms of Service. This is your business, so you should always read them. It is an investment in your future. Although it is true that most people skip the section where they have to agree to the Terms and Conditions, you should not do this. You should also be aware of any refund policies offered by web hosting providers.

Check to see if they have a backup plan. In the event of an emergency, you should always have a Plan B. Ask your web hosting company about the backup plans they have in place for you in the event that all of your site data is lost. If they don't give you a satisfactory answer, do not use their services. It's always safer to be safe than sorry.

Ask about security features. Security breaches can occur at any moment and to anyone. To be safe, ensure that your web host has taken all necessary precautions. Ask about their security measures and how they plan to protect their customers' private information.

Avoid new companies. There are no bad companies, but you need to be careful about what you put your trust in. Although new companies may offer great deals on their packages, they don't have the experience necessary to manage growth. If you trust them with web hosting, your site might suffer. It is always best to go with a reputable company for web hosting.

Check to see if they offer extra features - If you require additional features such as an SSL certificate or email host, you should check with the web hosting company before you make any decisions.

Whatever company you choose, ensure that your hosting plan supports WordPress. It is the most popular platform for building websites, and it is also the easiest to use.

Step 4 - Create Your Essential Website Pages

Your website is your strongest tool in affiliate marketing. It must be comprehensive and complete. After you've completed website hosting, you can start building your website. These pages form the foundation of an affiliate marketing website. Your first task is to create them. These pages are as follows:

About page - This page should be personal. This page will give visitors a sense of who you are and what you do. The popular belief is that the About page only focuses on the owner or author of the website. This is false. Your About page should focus on your ability to be useful to your readers, and your unique and reliable content. An About page should not be about your personal story in affiliate marketing. It is about converting your audience.

Your homepage - This page will be visible to your visitors from the moment they visit your website. This website's importance is obvious. It should be engaging. There are many themes available on WordPress to help you create a beautiful design for your homepage. It can also be a combination of your most recent reviews.

Contact page - This is where brands can reach you to discuss collaboration. If your readers have questions, this page will be their first stop. This page could be a great way to get some serious leads. It should also be simple to navigate. In case your audience wishes to follow you on social media, it is a good idea to keep these links up. The link to your Contact page should also be prominently displayed in the Navigation Menu so that visitors have no difficulty finding it.

Step 5: Write your first post

After you have completed the pages, you can start writing your first post. No matter what niche you choose, there are some posts that are very popular in affiliate marketing. Any of these posts can be used as a starting point.

These blog posts are the most popular. As an affiliate, you can create informative blog posts that show your readers how to use a product or how to do things within a budget. You could write something like "How to build smart homes under $100". This article can be written in two ways. You can either combine several products or focus on one product to give a comprehensive guide. Make sure the information you provide is easy to comprehend and easily read. Your guides should be able to answer the questions your audience may have.

Simple product reviews - Product reviews are a great way to get started with something simpler. Your rating system should be easy to understand and use. You must thoroughly research the product and discuss every aspect of it in your content. Your audience will trust your review if you are honest. Negative opinions are important, so don't be afraid to voice them.

Product comparisons - This is another popular type of article. They address the problem that every person faces when purchasing an item. Your article should focus on providing all details about the product that viewers could need. Your writing style should be informative and not promotional. Customers who are trying to decide between two products should find value in your writing.

Best of lists - These articles are about a specific category, such as the "Best Lipsticks of 2019". These articles should inform the public about the products currently in the top of their respective categories and the specialties that make them different.

It is possible to make your first video instead of a written article. People enjoy watching videos more than reading about them. It will be able to reach a broad audience.

These are the steps you need to follow in order for your website to bring in lots of traffic each month and generate sales.

Chapter 7: how to promote a product

Before you can promote a product, you need to become an Amazon associate/affiliate.

It's easy and free!

Approved

You can get an affiliate link for a product by doing the following:

After your application has been approved, log in to your Amazon associate account. Click on Amazon banners and Amazon links, then click on Add Product Links Now.

http://www.shoutmeloud.com/how-to-create-affiliate-link-for-amazon-product-tutorial.html

You can search for product name on Amazon and then copy the link to amazon associate which you'll use in your Youtube video description.

These videos will help you if you are still unsure of what to do.

https://goo.gl/aOpaIz

goo.gl/wnxpYx

Or, simply type it on YouTube.

Locating Products

It's now time to search for a product we can review and share on Youtube.

This one doesn't have to be complicated! We don't need to!

What I would do, is find a category I am already interested in and then look at it.

Bestsellers in this category

Amazon has hundreds of categories, so you can pick what you like.

After you have chosen yours, take a look at the top 100 to find what you are most interested in.

I chose the graphic and novel category

Since I love comic books.

I noticed that the Walking Dead Compendium occupied 3 of the top 6 positions.

These can be reviewed and promoted by me.

The price per item is $30, and if I promote them all, it would cost around $90. This will get me around $10 in commissions.

Promote an item with a minimum price of $50

If you are certain that your products can be used in conjunction with other products, you may also consider low-price products.

Make sure it's on the top seller list, and that people are buying it.

If I do my product reviews correctly, I am confident that this product will sell. However, I want to verify it with "hard facts a.ka." real numbers data."

You can do this best by using MERCHANTWORDS.COM

The cost of this tool is $30 per monthly, but you can get a 70% discount by typing "merchantwords 70% Off" into Google.

https://www.merchantwords.com/offer/january70off

This is not my link, and I am not affiliated with the company.

This tool was very helpful to me and I use it almost every single day.

This tool will give you an estimate on how many people are searching for that keyword.

Let's suppose I want to target TWD compendium Comics. I will simply search for it on Merchantwords to see if it is available for thousands of people.

Woot woot!

Take a look at the results!

Although this may not be true, I am still excited to see the thousands of searches that have been made for this product.

This means that there is an actual market for comics.

You can also search for other comics titles and get more keywords to target in my product review.

Because I want to target as many keywords possible, I will do this.

(Why? I'll make more money, duh!

Yup!

This is a huge market that I can target with these keywords.

After you have received the product, it is time to write a review.

Chapter 8: selecting your niche

If you're reading this article about affiliate marketing, I assume you want to make money online.

To increase your chances of success in affiliate marketing, you need a niche or focused blog. It is impossible to write about everything and expect to attract a targeted audience. Affiliate marketing blogs differ from reflection or diary style blogs. A clear topic or subject matter that is relevant to a specific audience is required. Only then will you be able to promote relevant and targeted offers to them.

Select a Niche You Have Established Expertise In

Although it is not necessary to be knowledgeable in a particular niche, it can help you establish credibility and influence. People sometimes dive into niches they don't know much about, based only on their money-making goals.

Online marketers who are just starting out often choose topics that have high search volumes over those they are proficient in. Your audience will quickly notice your lack of competence and switch to another source with more detailed/expert knowledge about the niche.

You can also combine your education and experience with the niche. If you have years of experience in the hospitality and travel industry, people will be more likely to pay attention to your reviews of hotels and travel recommendations than if they are studying child psychology.

Tip for choosing a niche: Choose a niche that shows a high level of competency to increase your chances of standing out from other blogs.

Let's say you see the nutrition and weight loss niche as highly lucrative. You jump on board like hundreds of other marketers, but you don't have any knowledge. Instead, you will rehash information already on the internet and not add your valuable input.

Passion is the Key

It is a tricky debate about passion versus money. Passion is key. If you don't feel passionate about the niche you won't have the energy or time to research and write. You will lose interest in the niche and give up.

Affiliate marketing is not a quick way to make a lot of money. Affiliate marketing is a long-term venture that will take time to show results. You can only sail through this journey if you are passionate about it.

There is another way to look at this stimulating debate. You can lose interest in niches that don't produce positive results, even if you're passionate about them.

If you begin to see small but encouraging results, you will be motivated to continue even if your passion isn't in a niche. Invariably, you will develop an interest and passion for a niche that can make you money.

But, I will root for a combination because it increases your chances at winning.

Passion allows you to see a niche from multiple perspectives. It's easier to think about a topic from different angles, even if outsourcing it.

You can rank higher in long tail keywords (three-to four keyword phrases that are specifically related to your products or services) if you focus on more topics. Longer and more extensive content gets higher views and social media shares.

Your enthusiasm for a topic is reflected in your content. This ultimately has an impact on website audience metrics like bounce rate, time spent on the site, pages read per session, and other such metrics.

These are the clinchers that will ultimately impact your search engine rankings.

Profits to Follow

You are not in this business for the money. It's possible to combine your knowledge with profits. Is it possible to make money from your knowledge of rare breeds? You can start to research niches on Google.

A Google search will show that there is a reasonable demand for this niche. There are plenty of ads. This is a sign that there's potential monetary value. It's also a sign that Amazon affiliates have a lot to make.

To determine your affiliate sales potential, get to the bottom. Do you plan to sell a few premium-value items or hundreds of low-cost products? A book on puppy training might bring in $5-7, but a course that teaches profitable gambling strategies may make you much more. Before you can decide on a niche, it is important to determine the types of products that you will sell.

You might want to start a website on luxury travel if you are planning to purchase more expensive items, such as luxury resorts or charter planes.

Reduce It

It helps you to dominate niches with a targeted audience. This eliminates the competition in larger niches and makes you the authority in the sub-niche. You're choosing to be a big fish rather than a small fish within a large pond.

If you feel that the travel industry is too saturated with big players competing for attention, you might look deeper to find a niche that has fewer resources, such as pet travel or gay tourism, volunteer tourism and babymoons.

You can be a one-stop shop for all things related to your travel niche.

If you feel the weight loss market is too crowded, you have options. You can choose to focus on post-pregnancy weight

Loss, weight loss for seniors, or nutrition for teens.

This niche selection strategy helps you to target long-tail keywords that are more specific and useful for affiliate marketing conversions.

Take a look around

You can find the most lucrative niches in many unlikely places. Sites like Reddit and Yahoo Answers offer a wealth of information. You can find a lot of information on the most pressing issues that people are facing and provide quick solutions. Flippa and other website marketplaces can be useful in finding niches that work.

A simple trip to the local magazine stand or store can provide you with a wealth of information about niches people are interested. You can find inspiration in a variety of niche periodicals. All the information you need is right there. To find the most lucrative niches, you just need to look around.

Are you looking for trends or something more permanent?

Another hot trend in affiliate marketing is this. Although seasoned marketers may be constantly trying to cash in on the latest trends, there are many people who are interested in niches and niches that will never go outof fashion.

Trend-based niches are typically topics that are hot, such as technology (probably latest iPhone), green living and games (Pokemon Go), tiny houses, and other current trends.

These niches are also known as evergreen niches and are always in demand by the internet community. There are many niches that relate to money, health, relationships and travel. These niches are timeless and never go out of fashion. No matter what the environment, people want more money, better health, happier relationships and more leisure activities.

If you're looking for quick and seasonal profits, hot niches can be great. Demand can reach its peak. But, once the niche is no longer in fashion, audience interest may fade. You can build your business for many years with an evergreen niche.

Some people love to launch tons of niche websites, make profits and close down shop before moving on to the next one. Others prefer to keep a steady blog that is an authority in their niche and build it into a long-term company.

Research is gold

Keyword research can be both tedious and enjoyable. It is possible to play with many keywords and niches, find topic ideas, and create tons of content inspiration.

Use Google's Keyword Tool as your keyword tool. You can check the global and local search volumes for certain keywords. It also allows you to find many related keywords (absolute silver) and the competitiveness of keywords. This is a valuable resource for online entrepreneurs who are looking for lucrative niches.

It is a good idea to start with any main keyword with a search volume greater than 1000 global exact matches searches per month. While some prefer keywords that have over 2,000 exact matches worldwide searches, others find 1,000 to be sufficient. Keywords that are highly in demand but not too competitive are desirable.

Let's say we search for the keyword "How to surf" on Google. This keyword may return close to 1,00,000. That's a lot of competition. Pay attention to the ads. It may be worth looking for niches if there are just a few of them, even after refreshing the page several times.

It all depends on your strategy. Some people like to dabble in niches that are highly competitive. Even if they only get a small portion of the profits, it's still a lot. Some prefer to dominate a niche that isn't well-known and make the majority of the profit.

You can check if any PPC (pay per click) advertisers are bidding on the keyword in Google Adwords. High competition may indicate high levels of activity and bidding. Keywords can have high organic search volume but low paid bidding. Depending on whether you're opting for paid or organic searches, it might be worth considering both before you move forward.

Let's look at another key phrase, "law of attraction". A Google search will return a few million results for this topic. However, it has very few PPC ads. It will likely struggle to rank on page one for the key phrase, with a few million pages of competition. However, you can still consider PPC ads.

To understand the pattern, take a look at Google's keyword suggestions provided by the Google Keyword Tool. Is the niche populated by people who are looking for low-cost eBooks, or free information? What do readers look for in this niche? Coaching programs Are you interested in courses?

Check the exact match search for "Law of Attraction" course. This niche is unlikely to have a match search that matches exactly 50.

Next, you can use Google Trends to study trends in the niche that interests you. Law of Attraction, for example, shows that it reached its peak in 2007, when Rhonda Byrne's The Secret made the theory popular. It has been in a downward spiral since then, so you might not be able build a lucrative blog around it.

Find Profitable Problems

This is not about making money off of the misery of others. It's about helping them improve their lives and still making decent profit for your time. There are many different problems that people face. Some people need to be more aggressive, while others are just looking for solutions.

What solutions are people looking for in this niche? If it is skin issues, do they seek natural solutions, quick-fix creams or creams? What is their preferred language for sharing their problems on forums? To make them feel comfortable, use the same words and phrases. These words and phrases can be used in sales copy or ads (more on that later). This will make your message more relevant to your target audience.

Chapter 9: promoting your affiliate product

Building traffic/followership

Your Customer and Marketplace base

Your affiliate marketing program will be successful if you can build your web traffic. The right content is key to success. Only useful content is what you want for your affiliate website. You can lose affiliate commission if your visitors don't find any useful commission when they visit your website.

Your chances of earning more affiliate income will increase if you publish valuable and useful content on your website. There is no need to compete to publish the best content. All you have to do is publish content that addresses the needs of your readers. If someone takes the time to read your content then they are more likely to click your affiliate link and purchase the product.

Use short tail and long tail keywords to your content. These keywords are keywords that refer to the product or its utility in your web content. Don't use sales pitches in your content. Instead, provide great information about the product and encourage people to purchase the product. Great content is the key ingredient in selling affiliate products. Here are some tips to help you get traffic to your affiliate pages.

How to use a product

How I used it

These are the results I achieved by using a product

This product is superior to all other products.

After you have created the content, you can close each page by inviting the reader to review the offer and then they will be able to access the affiliate offer on your website. Review the product and give tutorials. If your website does not get enough traffic, don't give up. Keep doing what you are doing until the traffic comes back.

How to get more visitors to your site and how to make affiliate offers

Guest posts can be written on the websites of your competitors where you think your potential customers may be.

Share your content regularly on social media. Don't just share once, share it as often as possible, especially if the content is relevant to your everyday problems.

Make a PDF file for free that can be downloaded and linked back to your website.

When you post new content, send an email newsletter or alert to your ad subscribers. This is a great way to create new email lists and keep in touch with your online visitors.

You should create similar pages on other websites and produce more content. As long as your website yields positive results, there is no limit to how many contents you can have.

To ensure that your links are working properly, make sure to check them all.

Promote your affiliate products by using your social media profiles

This could be the perfect time to register on social networks if you have not done so. You can market your affiliate products on the top social networks such as Instagram, Facebook, Twitter and LinkedIn. Here are some tips and tricks to help you market your affiliate products on social media.

#1: Don't promote, but focus on engagement

Your social media posts should not be too promotional. Instead, focus on the relevant content that will help your affiliate product solve their problem. For example, if you are promoting a tanning product, you need to write content about the dangers associated with not using tanning creams. Then, at the end, suggest products that offer the best results and protect skin from ultraviolet radiation.

#2: Make your videos and content more attractive

The best way to make money on your social networks is to use the same advertisement. You can, for example, share YouTube videos related to the products you promote on your Twitter, Instagram, and Facebook pages. You can also include YouTube video links in your Facebook and Twitter posts. This link sharing technique is very effective as it allows your followers to access all of your content regardless of the social network they use.

#3: Encourage your followers to sign up for your content

Encourage your social media followers to sign up for notifications and alerts when new content is published. You can ensure they don't miss any important information.

#4: Email notifications are old school, but still work

Email marketing is a great way to inform your followers about new offers and web content. In these email newsletters, you may also include promotional codes. You should ensure that your website visitors submit their email addresses so you can build your email list.

Chapter 10: content is everything

It is difficult to write an article for your blog. Your blog is one of the most important marketing tools you have for your affiliate marketing company. Your blog is more than a way to communicate with your customers and gain their trust. It also serves to promote the brand and educate about various products. It is the foundation for SEO, social media, lead generation, and SEO.

It is imperative to constantly publish engaging and valuable content. These tips will help you do that. It is not easy to write a blog post, especially if you are an affiliate blogger. This can be broken down into five steps to help you organize your work.

* Planning - Choose a topic, make a list, research, and verify the facts

* Title creation can be done after the content has been written.

* Write the post

* Add images

* Revision

Let's examine each phase individually.

Planning: Make sure that you have all the materials you will need before you start writing. Don't think planning is a waste. Preparing in advance can help you save a lot of time during the drafting phase. You will want to choose a topic that interests you or keeps you interested throughout the creation process. If you're able to choose a niche that interests you, this shouldn't be difficult. However, if you do not have a passion for the topic, it is important to ensure that you are interested enough to write about it.

Although blog posts about products that you market will be easier to write, it is still important to do your research to ensure they appeal to as many people as possible. You should do as much research and planning as you would on any other non-sales-related blog post. They will be what keep people coming back for more. Your regular readers will trust you more if your content is of high quality. This trust can be traded directly for sales and is a very valuable commodity.

It is crucial to organize your content so that it flows from the beginning. This means selecting a catchy title. A catchy title will grab readers' attention, but it should not exceed 65 characters. Otherwise, search results may cut it short. Most people will only read the title of your article and the introduction. The first paragraph of a blog post must be strong. Engaging readers can be done in many ways. You can tell a story, share solidarity with them, or provide interesting facts or data. Next, the first part of the article should describe the purpose and the approach you plan to take to solving the problem your readers are seeking.

Writing: After you have created a plan of what you want to write about, it is time to get down to work. Do not be afraid if you feel nervous about the blank spaces. Blog writing is a skill that can be improved with practice. Even if your first blog posts aren't perfect, it won't be long before someone reads them. There will be plenty of practice as you launch your site with 20-30 pieces of content. This will ensure that readers who have stumbled upon it will continue to visit the site.

It is important to remember that most people reading your content will do so via a mobile device. You will want to keep your paragraphs concise and to the point as most people won't be able to read through the whole post in one sitting. You will also want to include recaps and headings from time-to-time to show how the information below is related to the overall idea of the content.

The majority of readers are more visual these days, which means finding the right images for your content is crucial. They can also make text easier to read by breaking it up into smaller blocks, making it more visually appealing. You can use them to help lighten a dull article or make complex concepts more understandable, such as by using a graph or summary table.

Editing: Make sure to read through everything you write to make sure it is clear and concise. A well-written article is more credible and professional than one that contains errors. You should also check the structure of your article. Don't hesitate to delete any parts that don't fit with the rest. It is also important to make sure you have a clear call-to-action, whether it be to share the blog via Social Media or to buy the product.

This is a great opportunity to think about the key words that will bring people to your blog. Once you have a few key phrases in mind, you will want to use them in your blog. However, it is important that you do this in a natural way. A meta description is a description that describes the post. While it will not improve your SEO, it can bring you more pageviews.

Make sure your blog is a success

It takes time to build a blog that is successful. It takes a lot of hard work and dedication. You need to have a clear idea of what your blog will look like. But, more than that, you also need to be committed, attentive, prepared, and willing to work hard. Every day, thousands of blogs are created.

These blogs don't always last or sell. Low traffic can cause some blogs to "die" after a few months. Your blog can be successful if you use the right strategies and follow simple guidelines for how to manage and create your blog. You will also gain a reputation within the industry by having a blog that is well-maintained. Sooner or later you may be asked for consulting sessions on this topic. Here are some suggestions to make your blog a success.

Content is the king. It is tempting to copy content from other blogs if you're not a good writer. However, this temptation should be avoided at all cost, no matter how fascinating the topic. Plagiarized content is penalized by search engines. Search engines will reward originality and utility of your texts and, in the long-term, your web space will grow.

You can improve your website's position on search engines by publishing regular, detailed content (over 1500 words).

You don't have the skills to create content yourself so you might consider hiring freelance writers. Although you may be able to find people to write blog posts for $5 to $10 per post, it is not a good idea to hire too many writers. Your goal is to maintain a consistent voice throughout your content. While a couple of people is fine, more will cause more damage than good. If your readers discover that you don't create your content, they will be less likely to trust you.

When you start out, you should make a formal agreement to work with a freelancer whose content you like. It will make things easier for both of you as everyone will know what the expectations are for content and the timeframe. It is important that your writer agrees to a confidentiality agreement. If your blog gets noticed, it could be a serious loss of revenue.

A happy blog is an organized blog. To ensure your blog can be found easily, it is essential to use categories when setting up your site. WordPress makes it easy to organize your posts by creating categories. These are subfolders and folders that WordPress publishes. These are known as parent and child sub-categories. Follow these steps to take advantage of this system:

Click on the left sidebar to select Categories and Posts. Categories can be used later in menus and widgets. These categories can be used in menus or widgets, but they are not the same as the keyword label. This is something that you need to remember.

You will now need to name the category and create what is called a slug. Although it may sound strange, a URL-friendly version is what a slug does. It helps search engines find your posts more easily.

Next, create an add posts category. You will need to select the category that you wish to assign to the new post from the list. By going to the right and selecting Posts or All Posts, you can change the category for multiple posts at the same time. You can assign the posts, use Bulk Actions, and then apply the setting.

Engagement is crucial: Although you'll likely be busy creating quality content regularly, there are other things you need to do to make your results as profitable as possible. You will need to engage with your target audience so that they don't just see you as words on the screen. They see you as a person they can relate to and, ideally, help by purchasing promoted items.

You will want to make sure that comments are enabled on all your blogs and that you respond to any comments received on a regular basis. If you are asked for assistance, make sure to do your best to resolve the issue and let your audience know that they can contact you with any questions about your niche. You will almost always get additional conversions by doing a favor to a member in your audience.

Make sure your content is easy to share: You must ensure you create quality content regularly. Next, you need to make it as easy as possible to allow your audience to share your content with everyone and anyone they choose. You will want to display prominently placed social media sharing buttons at the top, bottom and call to actions asking your loyal readers for their help. You don't have to wait for WordPress to include this functionality.

Chapter 11: foolproof ways to promote affiliate offers

You now have a solid understanding of affiliate marketing, how it works, how you can increase your conversion rates and how to set up an affiliate marketing blog. How to choose winning products. How to minimize your chances of failure in affiliate marketing. You can do all you want, from high-ranking keywords to creating high-quality content to submitting articles everywhere and still not see the desired results.

Let's look at effective strategies to promote your affiliate offers among your target audience.

1. For each affiliate program you market, create a separate page to link to the doorway. You can link a page on your blog to the entry page. This is even better if you have a domain name to link each page.

2. Make sure you submit your site to every search engine. Many affiliate marketers neglect this step and lose a lot of traffic.

3. Make an eBook based upon the services or products you promote and market it. The eBook can be used to promote great offers. Keep it to a handful of good offers, and don't overdo it with affiliate links.

4. Email marketing is another powerful tool to promote your products and services to a targeted audience. MailChimp allows you to create a compelling promotional mail that is sent to over 2,000 recipients every month for free.

5. Run a Google Adwords campaign. Promoting affiliate marketing offers is easy with visual ads and video ads.

6. As many forums as you can within your niche. In your profile signature, include a link to your blog. To establish your authority and attract people to your blog,

leave informative, well-researched comments on relevant forums.

7. In exchange for your email address, you can offer free and well-written reports. Check out easyplr.com to see professionally written reports on many topics. You can send monthly newsletters to your mailing list and promote the most popular offers of the month through them. To get tons of signup leads from casual users, you can also offer a product giveaway.

8. Outreach. Reach out to influencers in your niche. You can also do round-ups with several niche influencers. These round-ups will be shared by their many thousand followers on social media. These round-up pages can contain powerful offers. You can reach out to beauty bloggers and get their top anti-aging tip. They are happy to share the link on their social networks for beauty, skincare and make-up enthusiasts.

14. Another great way to increase traffic to your blog posts is guest blogging. You can network with other influential people in your niche. You can suggest creating an informative and detailed post for your audience. Collaborate on other blogs. You can, for example, propose to create a post on top wedding gown trends 2017 for a popular blog that is related to weddings.

In your author bio, include links to your blog. People will visit your blog if they enjoy reading your posts (and there will be many readers if you choose a busy blog). Your goal is to be the authority in your field.

15. After you have made some profit, you can consider scaling up your business with Facebook or Google advertising. PPC ads can be used to get people to sign up for webinars, grow your email list, or just make more sales.

16. Software tools can make it easier and more accessible for you to promote your

offers on your blog. Skimlinks, a tool that converts existing business and product links in your posts into affiliate links, can help you save time and reduce effort. Skimlinks can also be used to find product references or recommendations and convert them into links that readers can buy from. This will help you monetize your blog posts.

Promote Affiliate Offers via Social Media

1. Before driving people to your blog, get them to interact with your social media followers/users. Social media with a lot of user activity, such as comments, likes, shares and comments, are considered to be strong social media. This is a sign that your social media accounts have strong social signals (or social proof). This is a sign that your social media accounts are receiving a lot of traction. This is important when it comes down to ranking pages on search engines.

Encourage readers to comment, like and share your posts in order to increase activity on your pages. To build long-lasting relationships, ensure that you respond to each comment left by readers. This will increase your reach and allow you to make repeat sales from customers. People will buy from people who are concerned about them, not robots.

People on social media love being told what actions they should take. People will respond to a picture of a kitten by liking, sharing, and commenting. You can now post the same image, but with a "Click like or share if you want to snuggle up with this cute kitten!" phrase.

You could say, "If you like dogs click like," "If you love kitties share" and "If you like both comment, even though it sounds corny." You can also ask for ideas. Name this adorable cat. These are audience interaction baits. It is as easy as putting a creative and well-thought bait in front of your audience.

2. Do not sell every time. It should be 80/20, which means that you only engage, entertain, or inform your audience 80% of time to make it easy for 20% of the time. Social networks are a great place to have fun and entertain yourself. Do not try to promote your offers in every post. If you feel it is necessary, include links sparingly.

Social media can be used to build trust, loyalty, and a reputation, rather than hard-selling affiliate products.

Social media is a place where you need to inform your audience about the benefits of the product, not just how it can be used. Overloaded feeds with sales pitches are not a good idea for social media users. They want useful, informative, and entertaining posts that are easily shared, liked, or benefited from by all. These posts should be about what they are most interested in. Include your affiliate links and share the post on your social networks. If you want to succeed in affiliate marketing on social media, keep the tone natural and empower your followers to make informed decisions.

3. Make sure to use graphics sparingly. Are we more comfortable reading periodicals that have images/visuals than those with endless text paragraphs? Your readers are no different. Promote your affiliate offer by using lots of beautiful images on your Facebook or Instagram pages. You can add humor to your posts by using gifs and memes as well as videos and infographics (such a Canva tool). Keep your followers interested by using both entertaining and informative imagery.

4. Pin affiliate links. Pinterest recently removed restrictions on adding affiliate links to pins. This opens up a new avenue for affiliate marketers looking to promote their products/services with stunning visuals.

Make a branding board that represents your blog/business. All images should be consistent with this persona. Users of

Pinterest should be able tell the purpose of your blog without having to dig too deep. Don't make people do extra work online. It will only hinder their ability to complete the desired action. Pin board titles should contain keywords. Make sure to fill every board with pins that you are certain your followers would be interested in.

Pin images of products and services that you wish to promote to a board you have created. If you are selling products related to men's grooming you might pin it to the Father's Day gifts board.

Next, click on the "edit this pin" option. You're done! Promote your pins via other social networks. You can also use the paid promoted pins option to promote specific pins using live affiliate links.

5. Complement industry influencers. The industry's top players can help you leverage a lot. You can simply create a post featuring them and have them share

it with your followers/fans. You can, for example, create a list of "Top 10 Food Bloggers Who've Inspire My Journey" or "10 Most Successful Bloggers For the Year" and send a message along with a link. The link will almost always be shared by the influencers with their followers.

This can help you build a following and convert high-quality visitors to your affiliate blog.

6. Refer your followers to your resource page. Share an affiliate link via social media. If this seems too bold and salesy, direct your followers to a separate Resources Page. Here you can promote hand-picked deals that you have personally used and benefited from. You could say, "Here are the tools I used to build my travel blog."

The host provider, themes and other tools can then be promoted. A resource list, such as "Top 10 Must-Have Resources for Creating a Beautiful Travel Blog" can be another tip. This list will highlight the top tools to help you create a travel blog, from stock images to autoresponders. People who have groups may ask for advice or recommendations on resources. Make use of this opportunity to get people to your blog.

7. Instead of creating business pages, create special interest groups or communities. If you have a blog about training dogs, you could create a group for pet owners or dog lovers. In a constant dialogue, pet owners and dog lovers can share their experiences and discuss issues related to their pets. Other dog owners can benefit from your expertise and offer suggestions. This can be a great way to foster a sense of belonging and a community before others buy from you.

8. Promote relevant posts on aggregators such as Quora and Reddit. These sites can be dangerous if you promote your blog. You shouldn't spam these sites to get useless backlinks. Only link to a post if it

answers the question directly or provides suggestions for questions that users have posted. Targeted traffic can help you reach users who are searching for the solution that you offer. These users are desperate for solutions and could be willing to buy your offer.

9. Hootsuite is a free tool that allows you to post links to your latest posts across multiple social media platforms in just a few clicks. To make it easier and more efficient, schedule posts ahead of time.

10. For affiliate marketing, you can host a live Facebook training. Here are some tips to help you get started. First, pick one product or service you would like to recommend to your audience. It should relate to the training and offer value.

Create a training script that revolves around the product/service you are selling. If you're promoting a course in social media marketing, for example, create a training topic about how to get the first 10,000 Facebook or Twitter followers. Limit the outline to just 3-5 key points. To make your link more appealing, you can use a tool like PrettyLink to cloak it. Cloaked and shorter links make it less spammy and offer more credibility to your audience.

To make the training unique and memorable, you should put as much of yourself into it as possible. You can add a lot of humor, humor, trivia, and statistics to the training. After the live broadcast ends, edit your video status to include the link. Now you have a training session which can be permanently referred with your affiliate link.

A bonus is a way to get people to buy through your link. You could offer a bonus, such as a digital or physical product, or an information report, free shipping, access to a private group, a coupon code, or a training session for no cost. Incentives work well with fence-sitters. For even more impact, set a deadline for the incentives. This will increase urgency and encourage people to buy the product/service via your link immediately.

11. Make an Instagram shop. If you do it correctly, there's a lot of money to make on Instagram. Although Instagram does not allow links to be included in posts, you can add a link directly to your profile or bio. Most bloggers will include a link on their blog or to their squeeze page. If you're a smart affiliate marketer, which I don't doubt, you may use this link only for a more resourceful reason.

You did it! You can even make an Instagram shop! You can create an Instagram shop! Before you use this strategy, check to see if your affiliate program allows you to link on Instagram images.

Add a link to PrettyLink to the rescue again in your bio. Refer to your bio link whenever you add an image to the shop. Add an affiliate link to every product or service you recommend. Visitors will be able view many of your products simultaneously on the shop. They can also click on images. Your unique affiliate link will automatically redirect them to the product page where they can make their purchase.

Promote Affiliate Offers with Paid Facebook Ads

When it comes to advertising affiliate products and services, Facebook ads offer a significant advantage over other paid advertising options. Marketers have access to large numbers of targeted audience members based on everything, from their hobbies to what magazines they read to what food they eat. Targeting people can be done based on their past life events, professions, and even their most recent travel destinations. Affiliates who are able to use the power of Facebook advertising can tap into this potential goldmine.

These are some tips from experts to market affiliate offers via Facebook's paid advertising option.

1. When selecting your audience, be specific about their gender, age, location, interests, and other demographics. Focusing your ads will result in a higher response rate. Your ad may not get the clicks you want, even if it does, the conversion rates will be low. You don't want to waste your money on a wider audience, even if it isn't focused enough.

2. Slideshows, infographics, and videos can help you communicate your message better. Split testing your ads with a maximum 6 different visuals is the best way to determine which one works. Facebook advertising is an excellent tool to test what works for your audience and which don't. A.png file is the ideal size for a Facebook ad. It should be 1200 x 628.

Bright, vibrant and high-resolution images will increase your appeal. A simple tip such as editing images with an app like Fotor to increase your ad conversion can make a big difference in your conversion rate. Avoid taking pictures that are unclear or too dim.

3. Your headlines are the core of your ad. A powerful headline should address the needs and interests of your target audience. It should also be able to evoke a conversation with them. The headline should not exceed 10-15 words and the ad body text should not exceed 90 symbols. To get readers to take the desired action, write a compelling Call-To-Action.

Ask questions about the interests or concerns of your target audience to keep your headlines interesting.

Statics can be a powerful way to grab their attention. Are you one of the 89% that suffer from stress-related sleep disorders? Get help

It should have a strong emotional appeal and be logical. One of the best and most reliable approaches is the problem-solution approach. Ask users to share a problem they are facing or present a solution. Your blog/page should be presented as a tool to help them solve their problem. If they are determined to solve the problem, encourage them to act. Remember the golden rule? Let them know what it is for them.

Are you tired of looking for the perfect waffle maker. More than 50 models have been reviewed. Order yours now.

3. Facebook gives you the option to place your ad in the desktop newsfeed or mobile feed. Selecting multiple options will confuse your testing plans so choose one option. A mobile news feed is a great option. If you want to direct users to your blog, make sure it is fully optimized.

4. For your ads, aim for a minimum of 1% click through rate (CTR). This is the sum of the number of clicks that your advertisement receives and the number of

impressions it has. Clicks/impressions =CTR. Your ads are performing well if it is higher than that. This simply means that your ads' layout, text, or appearance has struck a chord in your audience.

You can tweak your click through rates if they are below 1%. You can keep testing different versions of the ad until your ads are successful. Pay attention to the statistics. You should measure the number of clicks and the cost per Click for multiple ads. These insights will help you create profitable ads in the future.

5. To avoid overspending, set a daily budget to your ads. While you test, start with $5-20. After you have identified the winners, increase your budget.

6. This might not be considered a paid advertisement tip. You can increase the number of likes and fans for your page by activating your "Similar Page Suggestions". Facebook gives you similar page suggestions every time a user likes

another page or competitor. This can help you get some free likes. Check "Similar Pages Suggestions" on your settings page.

How do you come up with blog topics people love to share?

Social media traffic can be gained by creating great content that gets lots of likes, comments, and shares. A lot of traffic can be generated by engaging, detailed and well-written content. This can lead to a lot of social signals and blog activity. How can you make sure your blog is filled with content that everyone enjoys? Here's how it works.

1. Evernote is a note-based app that you should keep handy. While browsing your social media feeds or sitting in a café, you'll find tons of ideas for blog topics. Sometimes, the best ideas we have come across fade away. Make sure you keep track of your ideas so they don't disappear from your mind.

2. Use a website like Buzzsumo to search for your topic. The site will show you a list with the most popular topics in the niche. Then, you can create your blog post. You can add something to make it better than the original. Posts that are likely to go viral or be very popular can include affiliate links.

3. Keywordtool.io allows you to enter your primary keyword. This is where you should look for topic ideas and not search volume. You might enter "Hawaii Vacation Guide" to find related keywords like "Hawaii holiday scams", "Hawaii trip rentals", and many more. These clues can be used to help you create affiliate blog posts. These are the facts people actually want and can use.

Topics like "Top 10 Hawaiian Vacation Packages", "10 Best Travel Tips For Couples Planning a Vacation To Hawaii", "How to Find Affordable Hawaii Vacation Packages" and others can be created.

Google's auto-complete function will also help you discover many hidden topics. Make posts that are valuable. You can create posts like "10 Amazing Packing Tips While Going Camping" if you sell travel-related merchandise such as camping gear and bags.

4. You can find trending topics in your niche by entering hashtags like #hawaiivacation and #travelhawaii into social media searches. For inspiration, check out Pinterest.

You should look for topics that can be viewed from an unusual or unique angle. You might not find topics like "Top 10 Tourist Attractions In Hawaii" on every travel site. Instead, do some research and come up with something unique and unusual to share your posts.

There are many topic ideas available on Yahoo Answers and Hubspot as well as Reddit and Quora. This will help you to identify the type of questions being asked in your niche, and what solutions you can provide for them in your blog post. You might find that people are searching for the best apps for Hawaii vacationers. This will allow you to create a list with the top apps for Hawaii vacationers.

Chapter 12: affiliate marketing commonly used linguistics

To make a venture a success, it is important to have the right communication skills. Before you dive into any new venture, it is important to understand how the different parts of a business are called, what they mean, the words used by multiple stakeholders to communicate, and the code language.

Knowing the terms used in business can help you feel more confident when speaking with people who are associated with the company. This confidence will help you to succeed in your venture. You will be able to communicate the same language as the experts and increase your confidence.

This chapter will help you to understand the lingo and terms used in affiliate marketing. To facilitate natural searching, I have organized the phrases and words alphabetically. Here it is:

Above the fold – This is the section of the website/blog that a visitor can view without scrolling down. This is the section that loads first on a page.

Adware - Also known as spyware, it is a program that includes annoying and unnecessary advertisements. These programs can be difficult to uninstall, and can cause a lot of inconvenience for consumers. This deceitful advertising method is not something that established advertisers want to associate with.

Affiliate Agreement - A contract that you receive when you establish a new relationship between you and a merchant or affiliate network. It is a legally binding document that outlines the rules, regulations and responsibilities of both the advertiser and publisher. These terms define and oversee the affiliate relationship.

Affiliate Link - This unique link is provided by the advertiser at the beginning of the relationship. This unique connection uniquely identifies you to the advertiser whenever traffic is coming from your website and blog. This link allows you to track sales and traffic generated through your marketing efforts. This URL or affiliate link is embedded with the username and ID of the affiliate.

Affiliate Managers – These people help advertisers manage their affiliate program. They are responsible for recruiting affiliates and ensuring that affiliates promote their products and services. They act as a link between the member of the advertiser and the affiliate manager. They can be either in-house employees or provide services as a third party vendor, such as affiliate networks.

Affiliate Network - Third-party service providers who help advertisers manage their affiliate marketing campaigns are called Affiliate Networks. These systems connect the advertiser with the affiliates, increasing their reach. These systems also provide the necessary technological support to track, record, and deliver reports on traffic and sales generated leads by the publisher. They ensure that the publisher gets paid according to the contract.

Affiliate networks allow for both the publisher and advertiser to enhance their programs on a single platform. ClickBank, Amazon Associates and Commission Junction are some of the most highly rated affiliate networks in today's market.

Affiliate Program - This is a program where advertisers offer their products to publishers and they refer people to the services of the publisher. In return for referring people to their products and services, the advertiser pays a fixed commission to the publisher. Affiliate programs can also be called a partner, associate revenue, referral-sharing, or partnership program. Advertisers often use their in-house affiliate program which are referred to as "independent affiliate programmes".

Approval - Affiliates can be approved by either merchants or advertisers. The advertiser will review each application and decide whether to approve the affiliate's participation. Auto approval allows the advertiser to approve all affiliate applications immediately and automatically.

Banner Ad - These banner ads are visual, graphical advertisements of merchants that appear on the publisher's site.

Charge back - Sometimes, a customer you refer buys the advertiser's products or services but then cancels it later. Your commission may have been paid by the advertiser during the interim. The advertiser may have paid your commission during the interim. This is known as chargeback.

If the advertiser believes that the referrals were fraudulent, the affiliate program can trigger a chargeback.

Cloaking - This is the act of hiding affiliate tracking codes in links or hiding content on a website. While content hiding is against the norms, hiding tracking codes in links is a common practice in affiliate marketing. This allows for higher click counts and other marketing benefits.

Click Fraud: Many affiliate programs pay on a pay-per-click basis. Many people click on the link to make more money, but they don't have any interest in the products or services of the advertiser. Click fraud is the term used to describe fraudulent clicks that don't result in sales.

Commission - This refers to the money that the advertiser pays the affiliate for referring customers and generating sales leads. This is usually a predetermined amount that is paid to the advertiser if the desired outcome of the affiliate's marketing efforts is achieved. Sometimes, commissions can also be referred to customer bounty.

Contextual Link - A link that is embedded in your website's content, as opposed to being placed in the sidebar, which is a more traditional form.

Conversion - If a visitor to your site clicks on an advertiser's hyperlink and completes the required action plan (e.g. signing up for the advertiser website or purchasing a product), then it is considered a conversion. Conversions depend on the desired outcome and can vary from advertiser one advertiser to another. This element is often included in affiliate agreements.

Cookies - Although this term isn't exclusive to affiliate marketing it is used by programs that track and record sales and transactions from publisher domains. Cookies can be used to assign unique IDs for different users in order to track conversions and payments.

Here is an example of how cookies work. Let's say you have written a book review and provided a link to Amazon. A visitor looks at the book reviews and clicks the link to purchase the book. The transaction was not completed for some reason. The visitor finally makes the purchase. The cookie was already installed by Amazon to the visitor's computer after he or she clicked on the affiliate link. This means that you will receive a commission even though the sale was not attributed to you.

Cookie stuffing - This is an unwise way for unscrupulous affiliates to increase sales attributions. Without the user ever visiting the affiliate's site, cookies are sneakily and deliberately inserted from an advertiser's website to the consumer. This is done because the consumer will eventually visit the advertiser's website and make the purchase. The cookie would then be attributed back to the affiliate.

All legitimate users will not tolerate this type of underhand dealing. Affiliates of these types are also prohibited from many programs. It is important to be aware that such illegal dealings are possible and that there are methods to stop them. This type of affiliate marketing is not to be trusted!

CPA - Cost per acquisition/action is the full form of CPA. The publisher is paid by the advertiser based on qualifying actions taken by consumers who are directed to the publisher's site. Sign-ups and sales that have been completed are two common measures.

CPA, also known as CPO (Cost Per Order) or CPS(Cost Per Sale), refers to the amount that the advertiser pays to the publisher for each qualifying order or sale.

CPC - CPC is the full form of cost per click. It refers to the payment that the advertiser receives for each click on an online ad displayed on the publisher's website.

CPL – The CPL stands for cost per lead. It is, again, the full form of CPL. This is the amount that the advertiser pays to the publisher for each qualified point. These points could take the form of an email ID, completed registration forms or any other form as specified in the affiliate agreement.

CTR - Click-Through Ratio/Rate is the full form of CTR. It is used in direct selling advertising. This is the percentage of people who clicked on the advertiser link.

Datafeed - A file that contains all details about a specific advertiser's products. These details include images, descriptions, prices, and links to affiliate links. When you're creating an online store with affiliate products, Datafeed can be very useful.

Disclosure - This is a page or notice on your website that informs your visitors that you have been paid or compensated to buy products, endorse services, or make recommendations. Federal Trade Commission laws provide this information.

EPC - This is an acronym for Earnings Per click. It is the average amount of income that you earn as an affiliate per click. EPC is calculated by dividing the commission earned by the number of clicks made on an affiliate link. Let's say you earn $4000 in earnings over the lifetime of an affiliate membership. If the clicks total 12,000, the EPC is 33 cents.

First Click - This refers to the first step in an affiliate program. Let me give you an example to illustrate this concept. Let's say that a visitor visits your website and clicks on the advertiser link, but does not make the purchase. Let's suppose that the visitor visits another affiliate's site, clicks on the same advertiser link, and then makes the purchase.

The advertiser attributes the sale to you as the source of the advertiser's first click. This transaction must take place before the cookie expiry. Recall that the initial click to the merchant website was made from your site. You are entitled to attribution for the sale provided it occurs before the cookie expiry date.

Last click attribution - This is how an affiliate program works. This is the opposite to the first click. It is called previous click attribution. If any, the attribution for sale is given to the site that the consumer visited the most recently. The earlier clicks are ignored in this instance and only the affiliate site that was clicked on the advertiser's website is considered.

Impressions - The number of times that an ad appears on a page is called impression. One opinion is formed for each ad that is viewed.

Master Affiliate Network – A JavaScript code placed on your website allows you to link with any or all merchant affiliate programs via a master network. VigLink and SkimLinks are two examples of well-known master affiliate networks.

Niche - Websites that focus on a particular topic or vertical are known as niche sites. If your blog is about cooking, it could be considered a niche site.

Payment Threshold: Many advertisers require that affiliates accumulate a certain amount of money to be eligible for a commission payment. This is known as the payment threshold.

PPC – This payment model is also known as pay per click or CPC. It entails that an advertiser will make commissions for each click on an affiliate's ad. This payment model, also known as cost per click (or CPC), is used by many affiliate networks and advertisers.

ROAS - ROAS stands for Return on Advertising Spend. It is the term that is used to calculate the revenue earned for every dollar spent on advertising. This is the ratio that results from dividing the earned income by the costs of advertising and campaigns.

ROI - This is the full form of Return on Investment. This is simply calculated by comparing the profit or loss made to the amount of money that was invested in the business. The total amount invested would include the amounts spent on advertising, company setup, and other costs.

PPS and PPL are two common payment methods used in affiliate marketing.

Privacy Policy - Your website should have a page that explains how you deal with any private information they give you through contact forms or hidden tracking methods. This disclosure norm is required to be able to join many advertisers' affiliate programs. This disclosure norm is required to partner with Google Analytics or Google Adsense.

Super Affiliates – These are the highest-earning affiliates in an affiliate program. Usually, they contribute as much as 80% to total sales. Super affiliates are a favorite partner for advertisers as it allows them to concentrate on their core competencies. Affiliate marketing techniques work wonders!

Super Affiliates often enjoy the power and co-branding offered to them by merchants. The link from the affiliate links the visitor to the landing pages of the advertiser which contain the brand of both the member as well as the merchant.

Tracking code - This is the unique ID that you were given by the advertiser at the time you signed up for the affiliate agreement. This code is used to track traffic, sales and leads that you generate as an affiliate. It also determines which commission payments are made.

White Label - Some advertisers permit their products or services to be sold under the publisher's brand. The publisher gives the consumer the impression that the product is theirs. This is known as white labeling.

After you have read the basics, and some more, the next chapter will focus on how important it is to have a website or blog that attracts visitors to your site and increases traffic to your business.

Conclusion

After you've read the entire book, you'll have a complete understanding of affiliate marketing. You should now be ready to launch your own business. You will never be able start your business if you continue to think and rethink. Now is the best time to begin.

Affiliate marketing will allow you to make all the decisions. You will work for yourself and no one else. It is the most difficult part of affiliate marketing to create your content and strategies. Later phases are about reaping the rewards and tweaking as necessary. Affiliate marketing is a great way to make money. You don't actually create the products; you only sell them.

Affiliate marketing is about the audience. You must do all you can to satisfy your audience and offer real value through your content. Why would people come to you if they already have the content? It is important to be original and authentic. You should add your own personal touch to your posts.

To make your content more engaging and immersive, you can also create videos. It's hard to resist the lure of earning money while enjoying your vacation, or sipping coffee. Affiliate marketing can help you make your dream come true.